The Statue of Liberty

was given to the United States by the people of France as a gift
of friendship to celebrate the 100th anniversary of American
independence. At the time of the statue's construction,
very few children attended school. Instead, most worked on farms,
in stores, in mines, or in workshops.

Léo Fanch Ben Angus

The four heroes of this story—Léo, Fanch, Ben, and Angus—
each had his own exciting experience as he helped
to build one of the world's most famous landmarks.

✸   ✸   ✸

The extraordinary construction of the Statue of Liberty
began in France in 1875 and was completed eleven years later
on the other side of the Atlantic Ocean in New York. It took the
work of many people to make sure that to this very day,
Liberty would shine upon the world…

BUILDING LIBERTY

✴ A Statue Is Born ✴

BY SERGE HOCHAIN

NATIONAL GEOGRAPHIC

WASHINGTON, D.C.

LÉO PACIOLI

came with his family from Italy
to France to make a better life.
Now, it is 1879 and he is ready
to begin his apprenticeship.
His father, Angelo, has found
a wonderful place for him to work ...

"Léo, I have some big news for you," says Angelo. "Do you remember last year, when I contributed money to help build a gigantic statue called Liberty Enlightening the World?"

"Of course. You saved up for it."

"Well, I'd like you to meet my friend Simon. He's the assistant to the sculptor Frédéric-Auguste Bartholdi who will build the statue. And, guess what? He's going to take you to…"

"To see the statue?" asks Léo. "Let's go!"

On the way, Simon explains, "You'll be an apprentice in the workshop of Gaget, Gauthier and Company, the master metal-smiths. You're going to work on the statue."

"But remember," says Simon. "At the workshop, you will have to do everything the workers ask you to do, and fast! Go fetch a tool, bring something to drink, get another tool.…Be ready to jump as quick as a rabbit!"

"Wow! What a huge place!" says Léo, smiling in awe.
"We need lots of space," explains Simon. "Gaget's workshop only takes big projects: the Vendome column, the spire of Notre Dame, and the dome of the Paris Opera House. The Statue of Liberty is very complicated."

"We will need carpenters for woodwork and metalsmiths and blacksmiths for shaping iron, lead, and copper. And then pattern-makers and plasterers for reproducing and enlarging the model statue."

"Wow, this sounds like a really hard job!" says Léo.
"Don't worry. Just use your head. Think before jumping. Come on. To work!"

"Rabbit, two buckets of water!" yells a plasterer.
"Bring me the dividers!" orders another.
"Léo, some plaster for Jean! Hurry!"

"I'm coming, I'm coming,"
says Léo, running from one job
to another.

"Simon, how do we make this little statue so much bigger?" asks Léo.

"I use a divider to measure this small model and then I multiply each measurement," says Simon. "Using my calculations, the pattern-makers and the plasterers work a piece at a time to build the statue. Look, here comes our sculptor, Frédéric-Auguste Bertholdi. You should meet him."

"Ah, Léo! I have heard so much about your excellent work as an apprentice," says the sculptor. "Let me introduce you to our engineer, Gustave Eiffel."

"How do you do?" says Léo. "Are you the one who is going to pour the metal for the statue?"

"Pour? It won't be poured! It's going to be made of thin leaves of copper. We'll hammer the leaves onto wood molds made from the plaster sculpture. This way, the copper will be the same shape as the plaster statue."

"Then the copper pieces will be fastened with rivets to the beams of the iron frame that I've designed," says Eiffel. "After all, she's got to stand up, doesn't she?"

"Oh," says Léo. "The copper is like the skin and the iron frame is like the skeleton of Liberty."
"This Rabbit is as smart as a fox!" declares Eiffel.

It is now 1883, and Léo has grown up a bit. He's strong enough to work at the metalsmith's oven. "Hey, Rabbit," says one of the ironworkers. "Would you like to do a little bit of coppersmithing?

"I'll put this copper leaf on the oven so it will soften and be easier to hammer onto the mold. Come on, give it a try! Once you've shaped it, we'll harden it with some water."

The hammer is very heavy, but Léo pounds as hard as he can.

"Good job, Rabbit. You're doing great," says the hammersmith. "Are you coming with us tomorrow? It is July 14ᵗʰ, Bastille Day!"— The anniversary of the French Revolution.

The workers watch the parade from the bandstand, but what they really came to see is another statue…
"What a beautiful piece of work, the statue of the Republic of France!" says one of the men.
"Yes, look carefully, Rabbit," says another. "The sculptors have done well. But our Liberty shall be even more beautiful!"

Liberty is completed on November 30th, 1884. It seems as if all of Paris is in the crowd. Among the people participating in the ceremony is the famous French writer Victor Hugo with his granddaughter, Jeanne. Jeanne wants to go to the top of the statue, but the great writer is too old to climb all the steps.

Smiling, Simon asks Léo to take the little girl up.

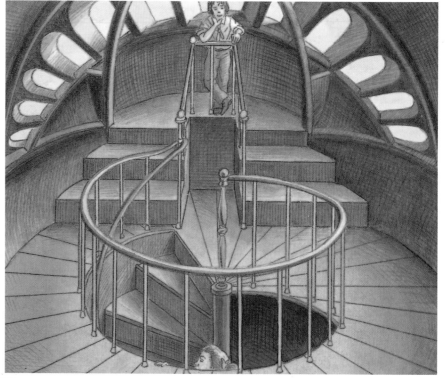

"Come on, Jeanne. You can do it!" urges Léo.
"Wait for me, Léo," she says, out of breath.

Jeanne shouts with excitement, "Wow! This is amazing. You can see all of Paris from up here. I know I'll never forget this day!"

Finally the time has come to take the statue apart and ship it to the United States.
"Don't be sad," Simon tells Léo. "Think of what a wonderful gift we have made.

"By the way, don't worry, it won't be your last project. Mr. Eiffel has not forgotten you. Soon you'll be a true coppersmith and make your father proud."
"I can't wait to be a coppersmith, but I'll never forget how I spent my apprenticeship—building Liberty."

FRANÇOIS PENHOËT,

called Fanch, was born on Groix Island,

near the town of Lorient in France.

When his parents died,

he went to work for the Navy.

In 1885, he is about to set out

on his first trip aboard the *Isère*,

a third-class freight steamship that is

crossing the Atlantic Ocean carrying

the pieces of the Statue of Liberty.

During May and June 1885,

Fanch keeps a log of his journey...

MAY 3ʳᵈ, 1885. Seventy train cars are bringing boxes to the pier where we are anchored. The captain has commanded all of his sailors to help with the loading.

The boxes are very heavy—anywhere from 170 to 6,000 pounds. Steam-powered cranes help, but it is still backbreaking work.

Altogether, our precious cargo comes close to 360,000 pounds!

I get to help my officer take notes for the inventory. After the boxes are weighed, we must verify all the labels.

MAY 10th. We're going with the head mechanic to the coal stations. We have to add another 140,000 pounds of coal to fuel the ship. This shouldn't be a problem for the *Isère*. She's a good, strong ship.

MAY 22ⁿᵈ. Today at lunch in the captain's dining room, my chief officer quoted a wonderful statement made by Édouard de Laboulaye, a friend of Mr. Bartholdi's: "Liberty holds a torch in one hand, not to set the world on fire but to shed light. In the other hand, she holds the tablets of the laws of the Republic."

Mr. Bartholdi and Mr. Gaget, who helped him build the statue, are on the ship. I showed them our boiler room where the men stoke the fires that keep the ship's engine going.

They want to see and know everything about the ship and how it works.
They ask an awful lot of questions.

Yesterday, I spent all day in the coal room where Liberty
is stored. I missed the departure ceremony.

MAY 27th. During a break, my officer told me all about the Sailor Code of Regulations. He says I must learn this book if I hope to continue as a sailor.

JUNE 6th. Yesterday, we hit a heavy storm. It was terrible! Things were falling everywhere and hitting the hull as the ship rolled and pitched. I was sick as a dog. My officer tried to comfort me by saying, "All real sailors have been seasick sometime. Don't believe anyone who says he's never been sick at sea."

JUNE 10th. My officer is very kind. Today, he showed me a drawing that he made when he was in diving school. I can't wait to be a real sailor one day.

JUNE 18th. We cleaned the ship today to get ready for New York. This is all so exciting!

JUNE 20ᵗʰ. We're finally entering New York Harbor. It seems as if the whole American Navy is here. More than 150 boats are escorting us. We can hear cannon salutes and the welcoming music of orchestras.

We are approaching Bedloe Island where the statue is to stand. All I can see is a sea of people—it is packed! People cheer. Sirens and trumpets blare. We're going to have to unload the statue, and then the workers will assemble it, piece by piece. And believe me, no mistakes allowed!

JUNE 22ⁿᵈ. I got permission to leave the ship and visit New York City. What an amazing place! The downtown buildings are very modern, and an elevated train runs full-speed among them.

JULY 1st. Today I saw an orchestra of children playing in the street. They are collecting money to pay for a pedestal for the statue. Independence Day is almost here, and everyone is getting ready for the day that celebrates the signing of the American Declaration of Independence from England. That date, July 4th, 1776, is even engraved on the tablets the statue carries in her hand.

JULY 2nd. It took us almost 10 days to unload everything, but we're finally done. Now we must sail back to France. I am so proud of the work I've done—carrying Liberty.

BENJAMIN LUTHERSON,
nicknamed Ben, is the grandchild
of slaves whose ancestors were brought
to the United States from Africa.
Now the Luthersons live in a poor
section of New York City called
Five Points. Ben has a job selling
newspapers for *The World*. As a newsboy,
his job requires a few special qualities—
good legs, a strong voice, common
sense, and an ability to persuade people
to adjust to new situations...

One glorious morning in March 1885, Ben stands on Wall Street shouting the top news headlines, hoping to get someone to buy a copy of his paper.

"Everyone needs to give! Help support the statue, or they'll send it back! Donate for the building of the pedestal!"

"The Statue of Liberty? No way!" says a man on the street. "Your terrible statue will attract bums from all over the world!"

"You should be happy that there are immigrants to live here and help build America!" yells Ben.

"I'll show you, you rotten kid!" threatens the man.

"Leave the child alone!" intervenes a lady.

"What's going on?" blares a policeman.

"Officer," says Ben, "isn't this the land of the free? Well, that guy doesn't seem to think so."

"Get going, kid!" says the policeman. "This is a nice neighborhood. You don't belong here. Go on! Get lost!"

Ben is furious. He shouts louder than ever:

"Shame on those who don't love liberty! Give as much as you can! *The World* publishes the names of all donors! Give your pennies, and read your name in the paper!"

When the workday is over, Ben looks forward to joining his friends for some fun. He heads for their favorite spot—behind the ferryboat station, on the construction site of the Brooklyn Bridge.

The workers let their children swim under the pillars that hold up the bridge. Ben's friends, dock workers' children, swim like fish and spend their time challenging each other to balance on the wood planks that float by from the site.

"Come on, Nick! You chicken!" cries out Bob.
"Come on, Ben! Let's go!" says Nick.
"Geronimo-o-o-o-o-o-o-o!" scream Ben and Nick as they take the big plunge.

Back in his neighborhood, Ben stops at the store. The grocer gives him a fish wrapped in newspaper, saying, "Tell your mother to pay her bill or else!"

Later, at home, Ben relaxes from his hard day and listens as his father sings a song to the family.

A few days later, Joseph Pulitzer, owner of *The World* newspaper, gathers some of his newsboys for a talk. Ben can tell by Mr. Pulitzer's face that the situation is serious.

"Boys, listen to me! I have just received a telegram. The statue has left France aboard the *Isère* and will be here in June…and we have only raised $50,000. We need twice as much to finish the pedestal.

"Tell the people that Liberty is not a present from the people of France to millionaires but a present from the French people to the American people!

"Tell them that the statue is the Statue of Peace, Respect, and Justice!
Be convincing! She needs you!"
The newsboys' jaws drop. But they resolve to do all they can.

Mr. Pulitzer must go to France to meet Mr. Bartholdi. He is
counting on the newsboys to get people to donate.

Ben is ready to do his part.

On the afternoon of June 6ᵗʰ, the subject on everyone's minds is still the statue.
Ben sees his friend Shoeshine Billy.

"Hey, Billy! Stop buffing—that shoe is beginning to
smoke!" says Ben.
"Hi there, Ben! You finished wasting our money yet?"
answers Billy.

"People in other states are giving money for
the cause," answers Ben. "It's the
millionaires who are not giving."

"Listen, kid," says the client. "Read other papers! Millionaires have given a lot of money. It's just not enough. Some people don't want to pay for it, others don't want the statue in New York, but in their own state instead. It's just not easy!"

"Yes, sir! You're right, but in the meantime I've got to sell my papers." And Ben leaves, shouting louder than ever: "Give freely! The statue is coming! It is almost here! Give your dollars! She's on her way."

By August, Ben is very happy.

"Liberty thanks the American people! Bravo!" cheers Ben. "We did it! We raised more than $100,000! Lady Liberty can now climb onto her pedestal!"

A passerby quickly snatches up a copy of the paper from Ben. "Thanks, kid. I can't wait to see her."

Ben continues on his route, thrilled at his part in the story—raising money for Liberty.

ANGUS DONEGAL

lives in New York, but his family
comes from Ireland. All the men
in his family have been firefighters,
but Angus doesn't want to follow
the family tradition. He works in
a completely different field, a new
way of building called ironwork.
In September 1886, Angus's skills
are needed at a construction site on
Bedloe Island...

Angus, a riveter, shows his family newspapers and magazine articles to explain his new job.
"Look, Arthur," he says to his brother. "In this newspaper, there is a drawing showing the iron structure and the stone and concrete pedestal of the Statue of Liberty."

"See," says Angus. "Eiffel's statue will fit perfectly on the stand Hunt designed."

"Who is Hunt?" asks Arthur.
"Richard Morris Hunt is the architect who designed the pedestal," explains Angus.

"And what if lightning hits the statue?" asks Angus's father.
"Take a look at this picture. The structure is very solid and tied to the ground with cables, so it can stand up against any lightning strike. They just poured the concrete for the pedestal. Why don't we go and see it?"

The next day, the Donegal family goes to Bedloe Island. The workers are busy installing the pillars and the beams. Thousands of pieces of the statue are scattered around the building site.

"Look at her little toe! It's bigger than I am," says Arthur.

"Here are the copper leaves that I fastened. The bars will now be bolted to the iron framework," says Angus.
"You know, Angus, I used to be sad that you didn't become a fireman like me," says Angus's father.

"But now I realize that it takes a lot of skill and hard work to do what you're doing."
"Thanks, Dad."

A few months later, Angus's father returns.
"Come on in, Dad," says Angus. "This is the workers' entrance."

"Have the stairs already been installed?" asks his dad.
"Not yet, Dad. But if climbing up the ladder makes a fireman tired, I can get you an elevator!" jokes Angus.

"What a view! Angus, I am so proud of you," says his dad. "Some construction site!"
"You haven't seen anything yet," says a worker nearby. "Soon there will be lots of buildings much taller than she is."

"Yeah, Dad, skyscrapers are the next big thing. Pretty soon, I'm gonna have even more rivets to lay," declares Angus excitedly.

By early October 1886, the statue is finished. Its opening ceremony will take place on October 26th, and then visitors will be swarming to see Liberty. The stairs reach all the way up to the head of the statue, and a ladder will allow visitors to climb up even farther—to the platform where the torch is.

Looking out over the harbor from the statue's torch, Angus enjoys for the last time the peace and quiet of the statue. Tears well up in his eyes. He is proud of his part—assembling Liberty.

The opening ceremony for the Statue of Liberty was a huge event with rousing speeches, lively banquets, and tremendous fireworks. Over the more than one hundred years since then, little by little, wind, rain, hail, snow, and sun have turned the reddish brown color of Liberty's copper skin a light blue-green. Thousands of immigrants have come to the shores of New York and gazed upon her as she welcomes them to America. Through good times and bad, she stands watch over us all.

"Give me your tired, your poor,
Your huddled masses yearning to breathe free,
The wretched refuse of your teeming shore,
Send these, the homeless, tempest-tossed to me:
I lift my lamp beside the golden door!"

—Emma Lazarus

from The New Colossus *engraved on the pedestal of the Statue of Liberty*

THE CONSTRUCTION OF LIBERTY

↪ 1. Sculptor Frédéric-Auguste Bartholdi drew sketches of the statue.

↩ 2. He made rough models in terra cotta (12–20 inches high).

↷ 3. Then he made the original model in plaster (4.5 feet high).

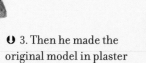

↶ 4. With a measuring divider, Bartholdi and the plasterers enlarged the statue three times. From 4.5 ft. to 9.5 ft., then to 38 ft., with the final statue to stand more than 152 ft. He drew horizontal lines to divide the statue into sections.

4xA

A

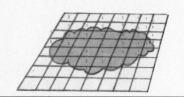

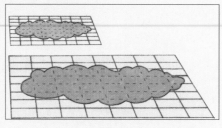

↑ 5. A draftsman traced the contour of each section on the grid of a huge piece of graph paper.

↑ 6. The grid was enlarged and traced on to the studio's floor.

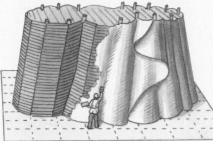

↑ 7. The carpenters built a frame and scaffolding made of wood. The plasterers reproduced a model of the statue at its final size.

↑ 8. When the plasterers completed a section, the carpenters made molds out of wood.

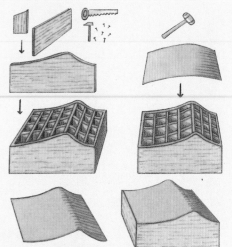

↑ 9. The coppersmiths heated the copper leaves to soften them. Then they laid them on the molds and hammered them down so that they clung to the shape of the mold.

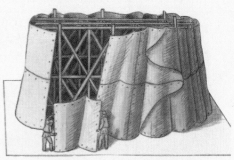

↑ 10. The leaves then entirely matched the shape of the plastered sections. They were assembled on a frame made of wood.

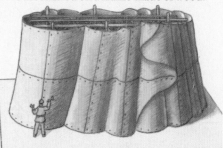

44

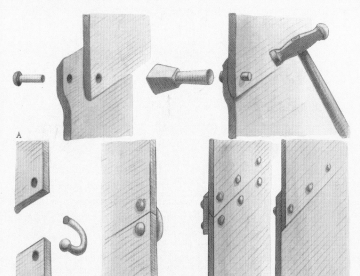

↻ 11. This is how the riveters assembled the leaves: A) one person placed the rivets into the holes and then another hammered the rivet heads down. B) Here you can see how the bent rivet was shaped. C) and D) show two other methods of assembling the layers.

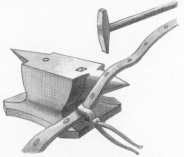

◑ 12. The blacksmiths shaped hot iron bars on their anvils. The bars became fittings that also followed the shape of the statue.

↻ 13. The fittings helped to stabilize the assembly of the copper leaves, but the leaves couldn't touch the fittings. When iron touches copper, it may cause a chemical reaction that makes the copper break down. In order to prevent this, a thin layer of asbestos was placed between the two metals, and the fittings were covered with a protective coat of paint.

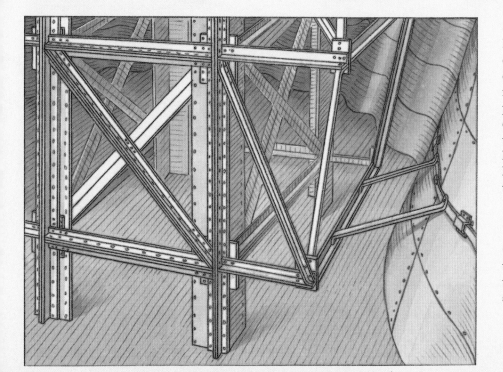

◑ 14. Gustave Eiffel and the engineer Maurice Koechlin were given the task of inventing and designing the skeleton of the statue. A) The spine was made of four iron pillars that formed the central pylon, or tower. B) The side view of the central pylon shows the beams on which the fittings and the copper leaves were hooked. C) A front view shows the beams that hold up the head, the arm that will hold the torch, and the tablets.

↻ 15. The fittings served two purposes: to hold the copper leaves together and to hold the copper skin onto the iron skeleton.

45

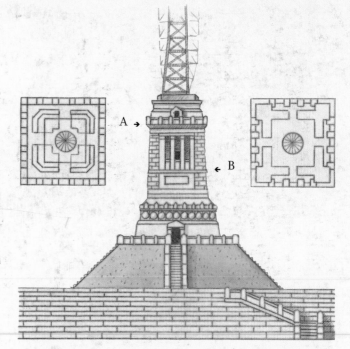

☊ 16. The architect Richard Morris Hunt drew some sketches of possible pedestals.

☊ 17. The architects completed the plans (views from the top) and elevations (view from the side), using their drawing pens, T-squares, right-angles, dividers, and rulers. The levels of plans A and B are marked on the elevation.

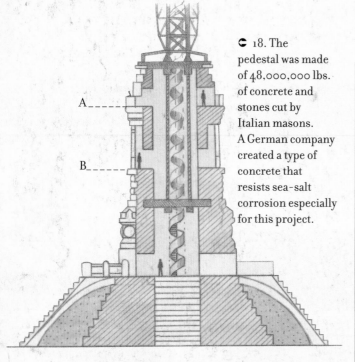

⟳ 18. The pedestal was made of 48,000,000 lbs. of concrete and stones cut by Italian masons. A German company created a type of concrete that resists sea-salt corrosion especially for this project.

"It will hold!" said Eiffel.

Despite Eiffel's assurance, the statue has needed to be restored several times. During the last restoration, done in 1983, French and American architects and engineers created a new staircase and a heating and ventilation system and reinforced the foundation. The acid contained in bird droppings had deteriorated the copper, parts of the feet had come loose, and a beam of Liberty's tiara had collapsed onto her arm. The old fittings were remade in stainless steel and ferrallium—metals that did not exist in Eiffel's time. Coppersmiths from the Champagne region of France even made a new torch that shines out over the harbor. Modern architects and engineers who have worked on the statue have only wanted one thing—to respect the spirit of the masterwork Bartholdi, Eiffel, and Hunt created while Building Liberty.

Copyright in original French version © 2003 L'Ecole des Loisirs, France. Originally published in France under the title "La Statue de la Liberté." Copyright in translated English version © 2004 National Geographic Society. Text was translated from French by Camilla Bozzoli. Further translation assistance was provided by Alice Murphy. Illustrations are in watercolors, pencil, and drybrush.

Published by the National Geographic Society. All rights reserved. Reproduction of the whole or any part of the contents without written permission from the publisher is strictly prohibited.

Text design by Bea Jackson. The book text is set in Filosofia Regular.

Library of Congress Cataloging-in-Publication Data
Hochain, Serge.
  Building Liberty : a statue is born / by Serge Hochain.
    p. cm.
ISBN: 0-7922-6765-6
Summary: Introduces young men who helped with the statue's construction either in France or later in the U.S.
  1. Statue of Liberty (New York, N.Y.)—History—Juvenile literature. 2. New York (N.Y.)—Buildings, structures, etc.—Juvenile literature. 3. Monuments—New York (State)—New York—Design and construction—Juvenile literature.
[1. Statue of Liberty (N.Y., N.Y.)] I. Title.
F128.64.L6H63 2004   974.7'1—dc22
                          2003018814

One of the world's largest nonprofit scientific and educational organizations, the National Geographic Society was founded in 1888 "for the increase and diffusion of geographic knowledge." Fulfilling this mission, the Society educates and inspires millions every day through its magazines, books, television programs, videos, maps and atlases, research grants, the National Geographic Bee, teacher workshops, and innovative classroom materials. The Society is supported through membership dues, charitable gifts, and income from the sale of its educational products. This support is vital to National Geographic's mission to increase global understanding and promote conservation of our planet through exploration, research, and education.

For more information, please call 1-800-NGS-LINE (647-5463) or write to the following address:

NATIONAL GEOGRAPHIC SOCIETY
1145 17th Street N.W.
Washington, D.C. 20036-4688 U.S.A.

Visit the Society's Web site:
www.nationalgeographic.com

Printed in Belgium